FRUIT OF THE SPIRIT

God's Code for Living

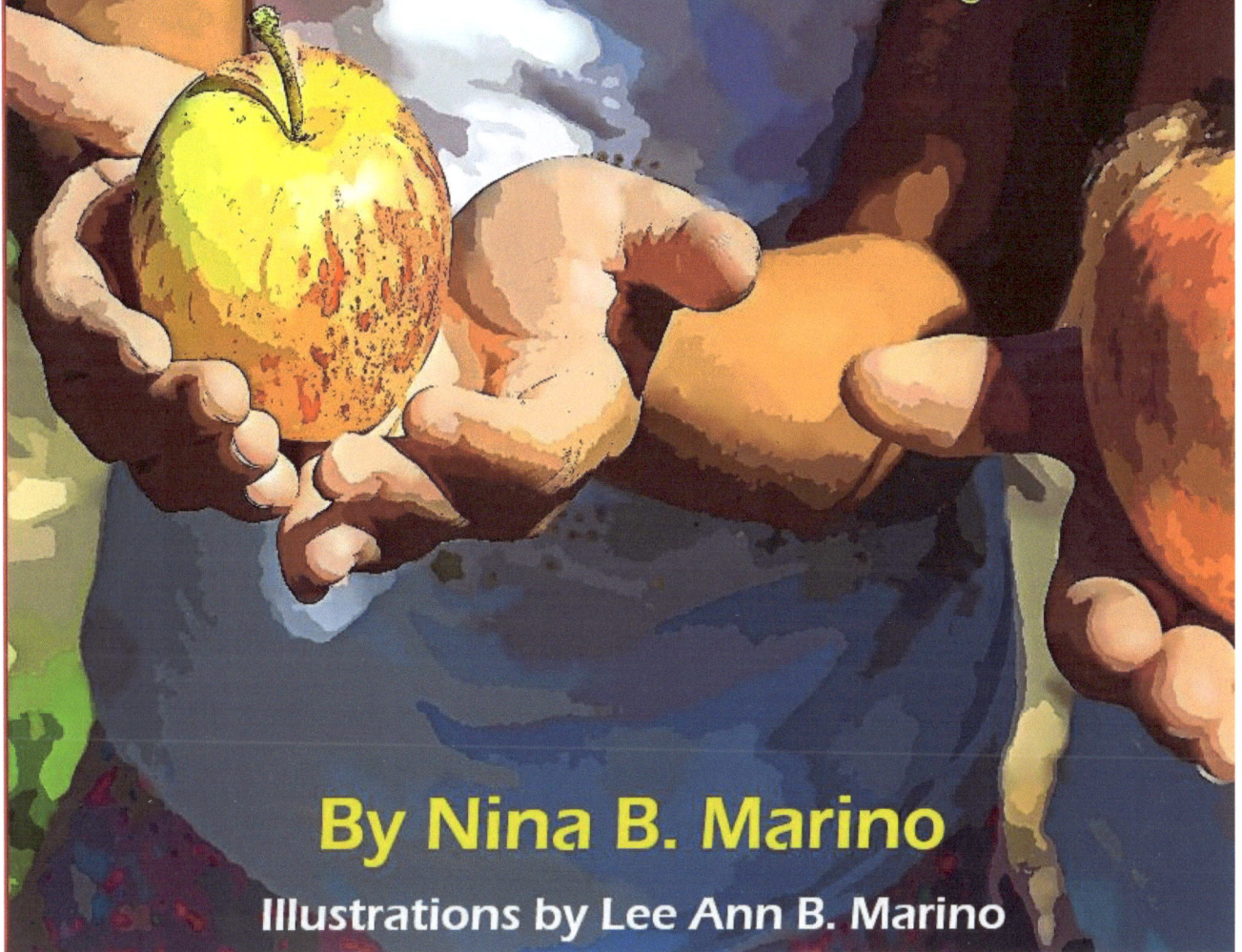

By Nina B. Marino

Illustrations by Lee Ann B. Marino

Fruit Of The Spirit

God's Code for Living

By Nina B. Marino

Illustrations by Lee Ann B. Marino

Published by:

Burning Bush Books
(An imprint of The Righteous Pen Publications Group)
www.righteouspenpublications.com

Scriptures quoted from the International Children's Bible®, copyright ©1986, 1988, 1999, 2015 by Tommy Nelson. Used by permission.

ISBN: 1-940197-58-9
13-Digit: 978-1-940197-58-6

Printed in the United States of America.

But the Spirit gives love, joy, peace, patience, kindness, goodness, faithfulness, gentleness, self-control. There is no law that says these things are wrong.
(Galatians 5:22-23)

F is for fruit of the Spirit, you see:

All working together in harmony.

R is for righteousness, for one and all!

The Spirit of goodness will help us stand tall!

U is for unity, kindness to behold,

so all of God's Word can be spread
and told.

I is for introspection, visions of self to explore

to make us feel better, with spiritual gifts galore!

T is for time, ever-moving and changing

with new chances to grow and times for maintaining.

O is for obvious of how great life will be

when we practice the fruit of the Spirit
For all the world to see!

F is for fruit of the Spirit, you see:

It is free for the picking for you and for me!

T is for time to practice our goals

for the fruit of the Spirit
will make us all whole.

H is for heaven, the place we all want to be

practicing the fruit of the Spirit is our guarantee!

E is for easy of how our life can be

with the fruit of the Spirit we will be set free!

S is for Spirit, God's code for living:

For our work in a world that is not into giving.

P is for Patience, long-suffering to wait

for a world free of conflict, that has closed all its gates.

I is for impatience – the far end from peace

in a world far from God, Who can bring
us relief.

R is for roughness, not gentle or kind

for a world full of people who just will not mind.

I is for instruments of God's love and peace

for His goodness, faithfulness, and spiritual beliefs.

T is for thankful, God's code to possess

for the joy that it brings, and never distress.

With the Fruit of the Spirit	**Without the fruit of the Spirit**
Love	Hate
Joy	Depression, sadness
Peace	Chaos
Patience	Anxiety
Kindness	Selfishness
Goodness	Greed
Faithfulness	Unfaithful
Gentleness	Lack of humility
Self-Control	Impulsive

<u>Prayer for the Fruit of the Spirit</u>

I pray to You, Holy Spirit, to help me find it within myself to always keep the gift of self-control, to always try to be patient and wait with dignity and courage, to accept what God expects of me with humility and all faithfulness. Help me keep my joy in every situation and never forget that love is what it's all about.
In Jesus' Name,
Amen.

ABOUT THE AUTHOR

Nina B. Marino was involved in the nursing profession for over 40 years and in legal nurse consulting for over 20 years. Nina also works and operates in Christian ministry. Within the Kingdom of God, Nina is a prophet and intercessor. She is an original founding member of Sanctuary International Fellowship Tabernacle (SIFT) first in Raleigh, and now in Charlotte, North Carolina, where she serves as an elder.

Nina has loved the written word for a long time, especially reading and sharing books with children. Her work with children has spanned as a mother, grandmother, school nurse, and childhood educator for well over 60 years. She loves crafting and cooking, studying the Scriptures, and working as a Sunday School teacher and in the church nursery. In her crafting work, she is a designer for Rose of Sharon Creations. To learn more about Nina, visit www.roseofsharoncreations.com.

ABOUT THE ILLUSTRATOR

Lee Ann B. Marino is a full-time minister, author, professor, editor, and publisher. She is author of over 35 books and serves as a licensed and ordained minister of the Gospel, serving in her own ministry, Sanctuary Apostolic Fellowship Empowerment (SAFE) Ministries. She is also founder of Sanctuary International Fellowship Tabernacle (SIFT), first in Raleigh, and now in Charlotte, North Carolina, and The Sanctuary Network. Within the Kingdom of God, Lee Ann serves in the Ephesians 4:11 ministry office of apostle.

She is host of the *Kingdom Now* podcast and also serves as Chancellor for Apostolic Covenant Theological Seminary (ACTS). She leads "Children's time" during Sunday service and also has a long history of authoring and designing curriculum for Sunday School, children's church, and Christian education. In her crafting work, she is a designer for Rose of Sharon Creations and in her publishing work, Editor-in-Chief for Righteous Pen Publications. To learn more about Lee Ann, visit www.kingdompowernow.org.

www.ingramcontent.com/pod-product-compliance
Lightning Source LLC
Chambersburg PA
CBHW041558040426
42447CB00002B/212

9 781940 197586